Thank You O Allah!

by **Ayesha bint Mahmood**
Illustrations by Asiya Clarke

THE ISLAMIC FOUNDATION

Dear little Muslim!

Allah is Most Kind!
Have you looked around?
His blessings you'll find!
Up in the sky
Or on the earth's floor,
Let's find out the things
To thank Allah for...

So let's thank Allah
For fruits that we pick,
For chocolate desserts
And lollies we lick.

And let's thank Allah
For giving us clothes,
For soft, woolly sweaters
And socks on our toes!

And let's thank Allah
For water we drink,
That pours from
the clouds
And runs in
our sink!

And let's thank Allah
For bringing the night,
A time to take rest
Before it's daylight.

And let's thank Allah
For sunny, bright rays,
As well as the rainfall!
Warm and wet days!

And let's thank Allah
For rivers that flow
For mountains and lakes
And fish down below!

And let's thank Allah
For big fruity trees,
For horses we ride
And honey from bees.

And let's thank Allah
For cows giving milk,
For sheep having wool
And worms making silk!

And let's thank Allah
For trips here and there,
In buses and cars
Or up in the air!

And let's thank Allah
For hands He gave – two,
And with our ten fingers
Great things we do!

And let's thank Allah
For giving us eyes,
The world we can see
Its colours and size.

And let's thank Allah
For both mum and dad,
Who love us and teach us
The good from the bad.

And let's thank Allah
For knowledge we learn,
For guidance and light
And good deeds we earn.

And let's thank Allah
For love of Islam,
Love of the Sunnah
And love of Qur'an.

"All Thanks are for Allah!"
Our lips impart,
We'll show Him our love
From deep in our heart...

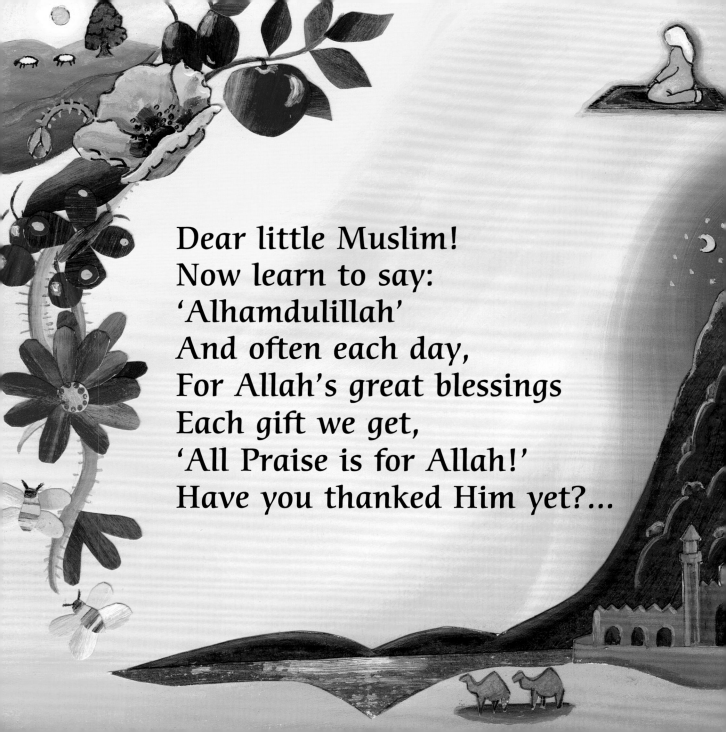

Dear little Muslim!
Now learn to say:
'Alhamdulillah'
And often each day,
For Allah's great blessings
Each gift we get,
'All Praise is for Allah!'
Have you thanked Him yet?...